BY COURTNE

I HOPE YOU
WRITE

how you feel

Introduction

Acknowledging how you feel isn't always easy.

It is like drawing a map, eager to get from one destination to the next, but with no guarantees or certainties that you'll take the road you intended to take.

Through my life, and writing poetry, I have come to realize that it is far easier to be there for someone else; to listen, to be a shoulder to cry on, to be the voice that tells them everything is going to be okay. The real struggle, is admitting how difficult it is to do the same for ourselves.

This journal was designed alongside my poetry book called I Hope You Stay. The purpose of this journal is to be used as a space that you can self-reflect and acknowledge your feelings. You can use this journal much like you would use a shoulder to cry on; or a friend to talk to. Whether you share your dreams or goals, your heartaches, worries or hopes; everything you feel deserves a space to heal and to grow.

As you make your way through this journal, you will notice it is split into sections, depending on how you are feeling. This is because we often feel things at different points in our lives.

If you are sad, write about being sad, if you are happy write about being happy, if you are angry, write about being angry and so on and so forth. You may find that you don't know how to answer some questions or that you are not ready to answer them, and that is okay.

Self-discovery and healing is a lifelong journey. Remember when drawing your map, it isn't so much about where you end up, but the road that you took, and that you were brave enough to begin.

All that matters in the end, is telling your story the way you want to tell it. So just know there isn't a right or wrong way to use this journal, and however you choose to use it, I hope you write how you feel.

All my love,
Courtney

A SPACE FOR YOUR HEARTACHE

ALL THIS BREAKING

AND ALL THIS ACHING

YET ALL THIS

RETURNING AND ALL

THIS LEARNING TOO

WHAT IS MAKING YOUR HEART ACHE? LET IT OUT BELOW.

BREATHE, BREATHE, BREATHE

WHAT ARE SOME THINGS THAT ALWAYS MAKE YOUR HEART FEEL BETTER?

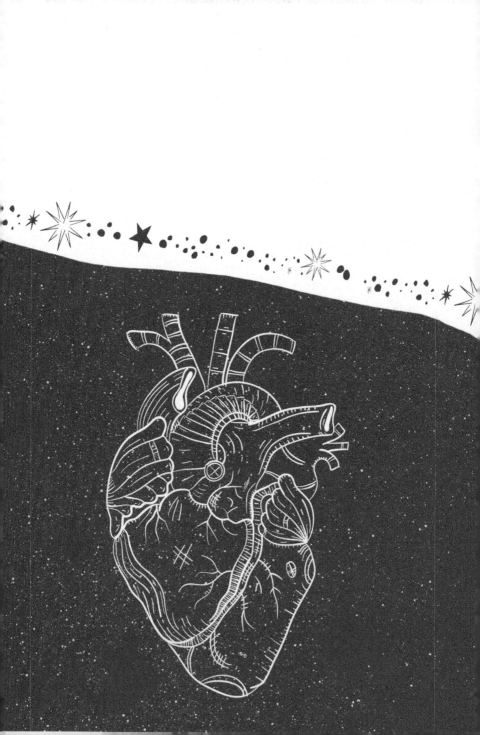

I KNOW THE FEAR INSIDE YOU MAKES YOU WEARY
THE WAY IT FORCES YOU TO QUESTION YOUR SOUL
BUT LEAN ON ME AND YOU WILL LEARN
YOU ARE SO MUCH MORE THAN YOU KNOW

SOMETIMES WE ARE AFRAID AND SO WE HOLD BACK.
WHAT ARE THE THINGS THAT HOLD YOU BACK? HOW CAN YOU SURVIVE THEM?

WHAT MAKES YOU FEEL LOVED AND SAFE?

DON'T BE AFRAID TO ASK FOR HELP THROUGH THE DARK

YOU DON'T HAVE TO CARRY THE ACHE ON YOUR SHOULDERS ALONE. WHO OR WHAT IS YOUR SUPPORT SYSTEM?

HEARTACHE CAN BE HEALED WITH SMALL STEPS. NAME A STEP YOU CAN TAKE TOMORROW.

EVERY MOMENT PASSES, THE GOOD, BUT ESPECIALLY THE BAD. WHAT ARE YOU LOOKING FORWARD TO?

A SPACE FOR YOUR DREAMS

WHAT HAVE YOU ALWAYS WANTED TO DO BUT HAVEN'T OUT OF FEAR? LIST HOW YOU CAN OVERCOME THOSE FEARS.

IF YOU COULD HAVE THREE DREAMS COME TRUE, WHAT WOULD THEY BE?

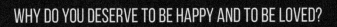

BEFORE YOU CLOSE YOUR EYES TO SLEEP, WHAT ARE YOU THINKING ABOUT? LEAVE THEM HERE. BE AT PEACE IN YOUR DREAMS.

DREAMS ALWAYS START WITH BELIEVING IN YOURSELF. IF YOU COULD DESCRIBE YOUR STRENGTHS TO A STRANGER, WHAT WOULD THEY BE?

A SPACE FOR YOUR
LOVE

WHAT ARE SOME THINGS THAT MAKE YOUR HEART RACE?

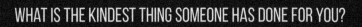

WHAT IS THE KINDEST THING SOMEONE HAS DONE FOR YOU?

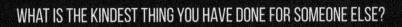

WHAT IS THE KINDEST THING YOU HAVE DONE FOR SOMEONE ELSE?

WHAT ARE ALL THE THINGS YOU LOVE ABOUT THE PERSON WHO HAS YOUR HEART?

YOU ARE STARDUST
MAGIC AND GOLD
AND YOU DESERVE
TO BE TOLD

WHAT DO YOU LOVE MOST ABOUT YOURSELF?

A SPACE FOR YOUR HEALING

WHAT ARE THE THINGS THAT BRING YOU THE MOST JOY?
SURROUND YOURSELF WITH THEM.

KNOWING WHEN TO BREATHE
IS THE FIRST STEP OF HEALING

THINK ABOUT THE THINGS THAT CURRENTLY BOTHER YOU. WRITE THEM BELOW. THEN, BREATHE IN, COUNT TO THREE AND EXHALE TO LET GO.

WHAT HAS BEEN ON YOUR MIND LATELY? HOW IS THIS AFFECTING YOU?

WRITE A THANK YOU NOTE TO SOMEONE YOU ARE GRATEFUL FOR.

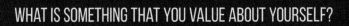

WHAT IS SOMETHING THAT YOU VALUE ABOUT YOURSELF?

A SPACE FOR YOUR GOALS

EVERYTHING STARTS WITH HABIT.
WHAT IS A HABIT YOU WANT TO IMPLEMENT IN YOUR LIFE?

HOW DO YOU CHALLENGE YOURSELF?

YOU ARE DOING JUST FINE

YOU CAN ACCOMPLISH EVERYTHING YOU SET YOUR MIND TO.
WHAT IS AN ACCOMPLISHMENT YOU ARE MOST PROUD OF?

YOU ARE ALLOWED TO STEP BACK AND TAKE DAYS OFF. WHAT IS YOUR SELF-CARE ROUTINE?

WHAT DOES SUCCESS MEAN TO YOU?

A SPACE FOR YOUR
STORY

WORDS, DESIGN & ARRANGEMENT
BY COURTNEY PEPPERNELL & WILDER

I HOPE YOU WRITE HOW YOU FEEL
© OF COURTNEY PEPPERNELL
ALL RIGHTS RESERVED. NO PART OF THIS BOOK
MAY BE REPRODUCED IN ANY FORM WITHOUT
WRITTEN PERMISSION FROM THE AUTHOR

www.courtneypeppernell.net

Join the community via the Pillow Thoughts app

follow the story on instagram:
@courtneypeppernell

ISBN: 9798608496738

Made in United States
Orlando, FL
05 December 2024

55003838R10065